5 PILLARS OF LASTING RELATIONSHIPS

SAMUEL DANIEL

TABLE OF CONTENTS

Everyone has a vacuum. This is why social connections are integral parts of human existence. They help to cushion our inward cravings for togetherness. Our interdependent nature makes relationships gold. Someone needs you just as much as you need someone.

In most cases, connecting with people isn't as tricky as maintaining relationships. Sometimes, an association can happen effortlessly. You could stumble at a fellow in a shopping mall or while waiting in a queue. Before long, you might develop friendship interests and share contacts.

Finding an intimate friend or destiny helper can sometimes be 'cheap,' but sustaining relationships requires deliberate extra effort. This is why character development is an essential key to unlocking lasting friendships.

It would help if you learned ethics to manage, sustain, and enjoy associating with people. This way, you can significantly minimize being a casualty in any relationship.

Regardless of the pain you endured in your previous relationships, dispelling the need for some level of intimacy will only intensify your aches. Instead of striving to survive loneliness, it is better to deck your life with relationship charms. You can master the rudiments of navigating varying levels of friendship.

This book, *"5 Pillars of Lasting Relationships,"* drums the timeless principles that form the foundation of lasting and profitable relationships in the readers' minds. It offers you practical insight and priceless wisdom to deepen your friendships, strengthen your marriage, or forge a more robust connection in your professional life.

Moreover, this book will help you watch out for the gems you must discover in anyone you wish to journey with. As you prepare to embark on relationships that are not only durable but enriching, you will learn the priceless principles of Communication, Trust, Mutual Respect, Shared Goals and Values, and Adaptability and Growth.

You are strongly advised to envision a better version of yourself as you prepare to actuate the power of genuine connection.

CHAPTER ONE

Effective Communication

Have you ever wondered why some relationships endure over time while others quickly fade away? Love, trust and compatibility play a role. Effective communication is the cornerstone of solid relationships. In this chapter, we will delve into the importance of communication in establishing and maintaining relationships.

As complex as social connections can be, effective communication is an element that binds every lasting relationship. It serves as the lifeblood of any relationship, encompassing how we convey our thoughts, emotions, desires and concerns to our partner.

Beyond conversational prowess, effective communication entails listening, understanding, and responding with empathy and respect. Active listening is crucial. It means engaging with the speaker, asking meaningful questions and clearing up misunderstandings.

Furthermore, effective communication requires expressing your thoughts and feelings in a non-confrontational manner.

Open, truthful, and respectful communication fosters a connection between individuals while promoting trust and averting misunderstandings that could result in conflict and break-up.

Effective communication consists of several components: carefully selecting words, clearly conveying intentions, and authentically expressing emotions.

Active Listening and Empathy

Sometimes, your friend, colleague, or spouse may only require you to listen as they pour out their emotions like an erupting volcano. If you are hasty to respond, you may ruin the communication process. It makes great sense that we have two ears and a mouth. This implies that we are designed to listen more and talk less.

Active listening involves paying rapt attention to what the other person is saying verbally or with gestures. Demonstrating that you value your partner's perspective creates a sense of connection and respect. One of the ways to achieve this is to let them have your ears and heart.

Listening and empathy are two sides of a coin. The latter goes beyond hearing to comprehension. It involves assuming the other person's position and experiencing their emotions from their point of view.

Empathy promotes compassion and helps friends or couples navigate challenging situations together.

Everyone gets more connected to those who listen to them with empathy. Since you'd love to receive attention, learn to listen to others too.

Nonverbal expressions like facial expressions, body language, and tone of voice convey a wealth of information. Responding with a gentle touch, warm smile, or supportive posture can express your intentions or concerns in no small way. So, effectively handling your nonverbal communication is an excellent medium for enhancing the emotional depth of your interactions and building a stronger connection.

Until you master the act of active listening, you might not know how much paying attention to your friend or spouse means to them. However, this may be challenging; you will need a lot of practice and dedication. I want to provide you with some essential tips to achieve this.

- Pay Rapt Attention: deal with every distraction and focus your gaze on the speaker.
- Use Gestures: Nod, keep eye contact, and respond to their body language to show engagement.

⊹ Seek Clarity: Ask questions to ensure you truly understand and demonstrate your listening intently.

⊹ Reflect and Paraphrase: summarize what your partner told you in your own words to ensure you understand their message correctly. Accept their feedback.

⊹ Avoid Interruptions: Don't be hasty to respond. Show maturity by allowing the speaker to finish their expressions before responding.

⊹ Be Empathetic, Don't Judge: Assume your partner's position and try to understand their point of view, even if you disagree.

⊹ Practice Regularly: Evaluate your progress by listening to friends, family members, and colleagues. This way, you can monitor your development.

Open and Honest Expression

Holistically, effective communication requires expressing emotions most healthily and constructively. Trying to suppress or deny your feelings can create distance and engender resentment. However, expressing yourself in the most appropriate manner can foster a higher level of intimacy.

Conversely, expressing a short temper or passive-aggression can damage your relationship. However, by learning to communicate emotions in a respectful and non-confrontational way, friends and spouses can create a safe space for vulnerability and emotional connection.

Without a doubt, open and honest expression leads to trust. When your partner feels safe and comfortable sharing their experiences, thoughts, and feelings without fear of judgment or rejection, they create an intimate ambience in which they can truly connect. This fosters a deep sense of vulnerability and allows them to forge an unbreakable bond.

What was your reaction the last time your friend or partner expressed their emotions to you? If your response hurts them, you might need more patience in relating with them.

Conversely, the last time your friend or spouse hurt you, did you express your feelings or bottle them up? If you bottle up pain, you need to be more honest about your true feelings.

Most of the time, the people who offend us are unaware of our pain. However, honest expression helps regulate emotions and provides an outlet for expressing feelings and experiences.

Bottling up or suppressing our emotions will result in a buildup and eventually manifest in unhealthy ways. But open and honest expression aids in processing our emotions healthily, reducing anxiety, and inhibiting emotional explosions.

By communicating openly and honestly, you and your friends, co-workers or partner can dig into the root causes of problems. Consequently, you can explore different perspectives and work collaboratively towards resolutions. This prevents conflicts from festering and enervating the relationship's stability.

Here are some practical tips for cultivating open and honest expression:

⊣ Select the Right Place and Time: Pick when you and your friend or spouse are relaxed and have ample time for a meaningful conversation. Choosing a comfortable and safe environment is essential to enable honest sharing. Be careful not to speak at a time when your partner is emotionally unstable.

⊣ Express Yourself from the Heart: Be honest and express your thoughts and feelings directly. However, avoid using ambiguous terms or beating around the bush.

⊣ Employ 'I' Statements: This technique will help you take ownership of your feelings, reducing the risk of shifting blame to your partner. Playing the blame game will hardly achieve a smooth conversation.

✦ Listen Actively: Pay attention to your partner's expression by giving them your undivided attention. Show empathy and try to understand their perspective, although you may disagree.

✦ Respect Boundaries: While open and honest expressions are vital, respecting your partner's privacy and boundaries is equally crucial. So, avoid pushing them to share more than they're willing or comfortable to disclose.

Conflict Resolution

Although conflicts can be uncomfortable or threatening, they are natural and inevitable parts of any healthy relationship. Regardless of how careful you are, differences in opinion, beliefs, or values will someday lead to conflict.

At times, our perceptions and opinions about issues may be divergent. It would be unhealthy to think that your partner is a demon at such a time. They are only expressing their humanity. However, you can navigate these inevitable clashes by learning how to manage conflict effectively.

Conflict resolution is not the same as avoiding disagreements or denying your feelings. Instead, it is approaching conflicts in the most constructive manner. It encompasses the willingness to listen, embrace compromise, and work together to strengthen your union. Conflict resolution can barricade misunderstandings and prevent minor disagreements from spiralling into major arguments if done correctly.

If you almost lose your temper, taking a relaxation break to regain your composure before addressing your differences might be helpful. Regardless of your hurt, learn to be open-minded when resolving conflict.

You must be willing to compromise and find solutions that work for both of you. It would help to adjust your initial position and consider unbiased solutions.

Contrary to some opinions, compromise is not about surrendering your values or beliefs, especially if they are right. Rather, it is simply about finding common ground where both partners' needs and perspectives are valued and treasured.

When your opinions or desires are divergent, consider the need to engage in open and honest discussions. You and your partner should highlight your stance, listen to each other's viewpoint, and be willing to adjust your position if necessary. The goal should be to reach an agreement that satisfies both of you without compromising your fundamental principles.

Every relationship runs on the fuel of commitment and sacrifice. If you must sacrifice your comfort or right to improve things, that is a great decision—and a wise decision, too. Every profitable relationship requires effort to run successfully; effective communication is the cornerstone. Let's proceed to the building blocks.

CHAPTER TWO

Trust

Every relationship- marriage, friendship, or business partnership- thrives when trust remains its nucleus. Trust is the foundation that sustains every viable and lasting relationship. It allows individuals to feel safe, secure, and valued in their relationships. Moreover, open, honest, and effective communication is fostered when trust is in place.

It is crucial to understand that as powerful as trust is, it engenders vulnerability. When you trust someone, you open up to them, revealing your true self, thoughts, feelings, and experiences. This high level of openness and transparency demands great courage and faith because it leaves you vulnerable to hurt and rejection. However, only through this vulnerability can we develop deep and meaningful connections with others.

Over time, I have counselled people not to sell off their trust cheaply to avoid regrets. There are two ways people become victims of trust. First, some people release their deepest secrets before verifying the identity of the person they share them with.

Second, people get emotional and swayed by deceptive but well-articulated utterances. This is why you must be careful of the information you divulge to someone who just came into your life.

Trust is a risk. So, you must be careful when releasing it.

Trust is built over time through consistent actions and behaviours. It is established when you keep your promises, follow through on your commitments, and demonstrate reliability and integrity to your partner.

Trust is strengthened through active listening, showing empathy and compassion, and responding with understanding and support to your partner. Over time, these small acts of trust-building add up, resulting in a strong bond between friends and spouses.

Maintaining Trust

It takes a lifetime to build trust. Never introduce betrayal into a relationship that begins with trust. The hurt is untold. When your path becomes shady, and the wheels of communication are detached, your partner could become overwhelmed with doubt. The bottom line is: don't just build trust; master how to sustain it.

Trust is a multifaceted concept that stretches beyond the borders of a mere five-letter word. Basically, there are five components that bind trust together, without which relationships become fragile and susceptible to doubt, resentment, and ultimately, dissolution.

First, **honesty.** This is the quality of being truthful and reliable in words and actions. It may take time for others to discover this attribute, especially with the high level of falsehood and deception pervading our world. However, honesty is indispensable in any relationship, as is the case with salt in any food. It is such a priceless quality that cannot be hidden.

Second, **confidentiality.** Your ability to maintain the privacy of personal information shared in confidence is what confidentiality entails. People have divulged secret details about their friends and spouses when a misunderstanding evolves. Such an attitude is deplorable and unhealthy in any relationship. It breaks down trust and opens your relationship to attacks.

Third, **accountability.** You are accountable when you take responsibility for your actions and admit mistakes. Most people think admitting errors will reduce them, but that's not true. Instead, it will foster trust. Moreover, learn to apologize when you are wrong. That is the greatest proof that you admit your mistake.

A boss will not become a slave because he apologizes, and a husband will not lose his headship for admitting his wrong to his wife. In fact, people who are quick to admit their fault and apologize are known to be more emotionally strong and stable than their defensive counterparts. Accountability signals strength and engenders trust. At least, you will be known for your flexibility.

Fourth, **consistency.** Being recognized for behaving in a manner that aligns with expectations and promises. A lack of this quality has caused many to lose highly profitable relationships. Business people who do not keep appointments with their clients will someday lose them. Spouses who fail their promises will be tagged liars even when they eventually mean what they say.

Everyone wants to work and walk with someone who always keeps to their words and promises. But people will detach from those who say what they don't mean but mean what they don't say. Never say 'yes' and act in disagreement.

Be consistent in your words, actions, and promises. If you fail a promise or appointment, be quick to give a reasonable explanation. That's a great way to win trust.

Fifth, **vulnerability.** It is sharing your partner's true emotions, experiences, and thoughts without fear of judgment or betrayal. By being vulnerable, you deepen your connection with them. Your ability to feel their pain, relate to their situation, and act with empathy makes their trust tank fuller.

Rebuilding Trust

Betrayal, lies, or even simple miscommunication can shatter trust. Consequently, the hurt, anger, and resentment can leave us questioning the very fabric of the relationship. It's essential to understand that rebuilding trust is not a quick fix but a patient and intentional journey.

I mentioned before that it takes a lifetime to build trust. So, you must be careful not to break it. One-time betrayal or infidelity is enough to cause irrevocable damage to any relationship. However, hope is not lost if you have fallen off the trust wagon.

Every skilled chef can salvage a dish gone wrong. Similarly, as you unlearn habits damaging to your relationship and cultivate those fostering genuine partnership, you can rebuild trust and bring back the sweetness of a relationship. I will share some practical ways to restore trust.

⁕ Acknowledge the Pain: Often, it is crucial to acknowledge the pain caused by the breach. Admit your actions and the impact they had on your partner. Avoid making excuses or attempting to minimize the hurt.

⊹ Sincere Apology: A genuine apology is crucial for showing true remorse. Take responsibility for your actions and express your commitment to making amends where necessary.

⊹ Be Transparent: Transparency is very vital for restoring trust. Communicate your thoughts, feelings, and motivations with high openness and honesty. Share your intentions and be willing to provide answers to any questions your partner may have.

⊹ Show Consistency: "Actions speak louder than words," they say. Let your partner see your genuine commitment to rebuilding trust through consistent behaviour that resonates with your promises.

⊹ Patience and Forgiveness: Rebuilding trust does not occur spontaneously; it requires time and effort. You have to exercise patience with yourself and your partner. Forgiveness is a process that requires a willingness to let go of the past and focus on moving forward together.

⊹ Seek External Support: If the need arises, consider a counsellor's support or seek help from someone you trust. They can guide you to develop strategies for healthily rebuilding trust.

While rebuilding trust, it is important to be patient with your partner as they heal from the breach. Remember that healing is a process. They may lack interest or refuse to communicate for some time, but you have to remain consistent with your resolution to effect a positive change.

Don't bother about it if you cannot win their trust anymore. You have learned your lessons but shouldn't pitch a tent with guilt. Sooner or later, they will realize you are a changed person. Even if they fail to look in your direction, yesterday is gone, but tomorrow is yours to win. You can set a new template for your new relationships.

CHAPTER THREE

Mutual Respect

One of the most significant yet overlooked elements of longevity and happiness in any relationship is mutual respect. It encompasses acknowledging and appreciating an individual's differences, feelings, beliefs, and values, even if they diverge from yours.

Mutual respect means acknowledging your partner's inherent worth. This acknowledgement is further reflected in how you treat them with consideration, kindness, and understanding. Without regard for individual differences, every relationship is like a house built on shifting sand. It will eventually crumble.

Abuse, assault, resentment, and constant arguments are signals that mutual respect is lacking in a relationship. As expected, such vices lead to disharmony and, ultimately, dissolution.

Several promising relationships have been ruined due to tenacity to ego. When both parties in a relationship do not embrace compromise, they will hardly manage their union effectively. But where individuals are assured of acceptance, they unleash their best to make things work.

If you are such that flag down your spouse or friend, you may need to adjust. Speaking harsh words, emotional or physical abuse, and public and disgraceful rebukes are all different ways of expressing disrespect. Regardless of your companion's actions, you can choose how to respond.

Especially in marriage, the greatest relationship between a man and a woman is fulfilment, which is highly conditioned. Where mutual respect is frictional, relationships wear out quickly. This happens when the value of one of both parties in the union is undermined.

Mutual respect cannot be toyed with, even in a relationship where one party is greater than the other in rank. For instance, a boss should respect his subordinates. If they all back out for being treated with contempt, you will get stripped of your title.

The best way to demand respect is to earn it by portraying a good example. You will hardly get disrespected for regarding and esteeming others rightly. If you want to honour, communicate it by honouring others. Anyone who keeps fighting for respect is not worth it. Do you want more respect? Then, show more respect.

Sometimes, you could also find yourself in a relationship with someone with high disregard. Maybe they have a character defect. However, the best way to correct this is by showing good examples. Fighting with them has two implications: first, it will ruin your relationship, and second, they will likely not change.

Understanding that we need one another regardless of our social, economic, or political status should foster mutual respect. This would allow your relationship with a friend or spouse to become more intimate and long-lasting.

Valuing Differences

Enduring love does not connote sameness but acknowledging, accepting, and celebrating differences. Every vibrant and resilient relationship is a blend of diverse experiences, backgrounds, and personalities that each individual brings.

The bedrock of a meaningful and flourishing relationship is a good understanding and affection for each other's unique perspectives, odds, and dreams.

Relationships bubble when there is unity in diversity. You can improve through synergy when you value and accept your partner's differences. Moreover, you have the opportunity to complement yourself. It's colourful when two partners can cover up each other's weaknesses.

It's easy to be drawn to someone who shares our interests and values, but the true connection goes deeper. It involves acknowledging and valuing the things that make our partner different. Those differences might include communication styles, interests and hobbies, values, and beliefs. Your political viewpoints, religious beliefs, or approaches to parenting might differ, but learn to accommodate your spouse's perspectives.

Instead of seeing differences as obstacles, envision and appreciate their richness. Each difference offers an opportunity for growth, emotional maturity, and a deeper understanding of the world. So, you can show great respect to your partner by not forcing them to accept your opinions and standards alone.

The next time you encounter a disagreement with your partner, reflect on their unique contribution to the overall beauty and strength of the relationship. This is how we build a foundation for passionate and enduring love.

Support and Encouragement

Support in a relationship can take many forms. It can mean providing emotional support during difficult times, offering practical help and assistance when needed, or simply being there to listen and offer a word of consolation and advice.

By supporting your partner, you create a safe and secure environment where you both can grow and thrive as individuals or as a couple.

On the other hand, encouragement is about helping each other reach your full potential. It means celebrating each other's successes and offering encouragement and motivation when faced with challenges. You can also create opportunities for growth and development. Encouraging each other creates a positive and enabling ambience that supports personal and relational growth.

I know a man who would make his wife go bankrupt because he wants to prevent her from getting richer than him. This fellow would borrow a large sum from his wife's capital and cunningly refuse to refund. Such a competitive spirit kills relationships faster than mortal combat.

Support and encouragement are crucial for building an enduring relationship. They play complementary roles. Support creates a safe and enabling atmosphere for growth and development. Encouragement, on the other hand, helps partners attain their full potential. It empowers them to become the best versions of themselves.

You will get the credit if you help your spouse or friend rise. Never be the reason your partner's potential will remain untapped. You will do yourself more harm by attempting such.

If your partner is facing a challenge or going through a difficult time, offer to help in any way you can. This could mean helping with some house chores if you're married or providing emotional support. These small acts of kindness can go a long way in showing your partner that you care.

Another vital way to strengthen your partner is to celebrate successes and milestones together! Offer soul-lifting words and show your excitement and pride in their accomplishments. Instead of being envious of your partner's new feat, strengthen your bond by rejoicing with them.

Again, you can create opportunities for growth and development. Encourage your partner to pursue their passions and interests, and support their efforts.

This could mean taking a class together, attending a conference, or simply encouraging them to try something new. When partners grow together, they grease their relationship and reduce friction.

Please understand that patience and understanding are crucial. Building an enduring relationship takes time and effort. There will be challenges and setbacks, but remaining patient and understanding is essential. Offer support and encouragement, and work together to find solutions.

Every relationship that will thrive must respect boundaries. Boundaries exist in a marriage relationship where the man and his wife are esteemed as one. Oneness is not a license to mistreat your spouse. It is the more reason you have to honour them.

Although they are invisible lines, boundaries define the limits of acceptable behaviour and expectations. They ensure your partner's needs and well-being are respected.

Boundaries come in various forms: physical, emotional, intellectual, and sexual. They establish a safe and comfortable space where individuals feel respected and protected.

Physical boundaries, for instance, include personal space, touch, and privacy, while emotional boundaries protect feelings, thoughts, and values. Intellectual boundaries, on the other hand, safeguard beliefs, opinions, and personal growth, while sexual boundaries highlight acceptable behaviours and preferences.

Allow your partner time and space to pursue their interests. Do not take it personally if they need time to stay alone for a bit of time. This is especially true for friendships. However, spouses should be careful not to subject their partners to emotional torture by choosing a long time off. If you are uncomfortable with any decision from your spouse, you can discuss it and reach a consensus.

Importantly, avoid pushing your partner's emotional buttons or trying to manipulate their feelings. Respect their need for privacy and autonomy. Recognize that your partner is a unique individual with their thoughts, beliefs, and experiences. Avoid trying to change them forcefully. Instead, support their individuality until you achieve a common ground.

You usually enjoy your relationship more by honouring boundaries than breaking them. Remember that boundaries are not a sign of selfishness or weakness; they are a foundation for healthy and respectful relationships.

CHAPTER FOUR

Shared Goals and Values

Imagine two people who, despite being passionate about different things, share the ambition of building a business or raising a family together. This shared vision binds the duo and instils the desire for corporate success. Shared goals foster collaboration, encourage compromise and motivate genuine partnership.

You need to find common ground with your partner. Your shared vision will fuel a lasting journey. With set goals, relationships become meaningful and transparent.

In any kind of relationship- professional or marriage- when goals are shared, the journey becomes less about individual fulfilment and more about collective achievement. This shared sense of purpose strengthens the relationship and fosters togetherness.

Never associate with someone with no direction or goal in pursuit. Have you ever wondered why affairs don't last? It is because the goal is an aimless one. That seems paradoxical, right?

Any relationship built on sexual gratification has its foundation in shifting sand. It won't take long before it collapses. Sex is never a goal; it only consummates marriage. Vision and purpose are the bedrock of enduring relationships.

Ensure you have clearly defined goals and values in any relationship journey you wish to embark on. They will serve as your compass when the going gets tough.

Creating Life Goals

Goal-setting is a powerful tool for both personal and corporate growth and development. It will provide a roadmap for your union. Moreover, it will help you to focus your efforts and resources on what truly matters to your advancement.

One of the most potent ways that life goals can foster enduring relationships is by providing a shared purpose. When two people have a common goal, they are naturally drawn to each other. So they won't lack support and encouragement for the journey.

Whether building a family, starting a business, or learning a new skill, shared goals can help create a sense of connection and intimacy.

By setting life goals, you are articulating your values and priorities. This can be an excellent way to ensure you progress toward purpose fulfilment.

Discussing your goals with your partner lets you learn more about their passions and aspirations. This will undoubtedly help you understand each other on a deeper level.

These experiences are rich and rewarding and can help you build a stronger sense of self. As you grow and develop, you will become a more exciting and engaging partner to your friends or spouse.

Setting life goals is committing to your partner to achieve something specific. This can help you stay accountable, as you have a clear target for which to aim. By involving your partner in your goal-setting process, they can motivate and monitor your progress.

Always celebrate your success with your spouse when you achieve a life goal. Celebrating a new feat is a powerful way to motivate you to attempt more significant tasks.

Take the time to acknowledge your success, whether a small victory or a significant milestone. Acknowledging your success is an excellent way to show your partner some appreciation for their support. Plus, it will help create a sense of connection and intimacy. Regrettably, some people miss this vital part. They want to shut everyone out after achieving an incredible feat.

But you need to realize that there are several milestones to accomplish. As you feature your friends or spouse in your success stories, they will support you more and more.

Navigating Differences

Sometimes, setting goals and values does not necessarily mean that you share your opinion with your friend or spouse. Passions can sometimes differ. It is better to journey with someone who shares your passions.

However, if you find later that your passion differs from your spouse's, divorce isn't the solution. You can navigate your differences and find common ground.

The first step to navigating value differences is acknowledging and respecting that individuals hold different values. Avoid dismissing or demeaning your friend or spouse's values simply because they differ from yours. Instead, take the time to understand and appreciate the perspectives and experiences shaping their beliefs.

Try to understand their perspective, even if you do not share it. Plug yourself into their experiences and feelings to build a bridge of understanding. Sometimes, all you need to establish a consensus is to accept and honour your partner's differences.

While it may not always be possible to agree with someone's values fully, focus on finding areas of common ground. Identify interests or values that both of you can agree on. This can lay the positive foundation for a relationship that will stand the test of time.

Importantly, be mindful of the language you use when discussing value differences. Avoid using judgmental or accusatory terms. Instead, choose a respectful language that conveys your understanding, open mind, and willingness to engage in dialogue.

It may be necessary to compromise or find a middle ground in certain situations. This does not mean abandoning your values but finding a solution that addresses the concerns of both parties. Be willing to negotiate and explore creative solutions, but remember that your partner's perspectives are equally important.

CHAPTER FIVE

Adaptability and Growth

Life is full of inevitable and sometimes expected twists and turns. Change always occurs, from career changes to family crises to the ebbing flow of personal growth. Envisaging an enduring relationship should spur preparations for coping with these changes.

Even though we don't desire unpleasant situations, it is wise to prepare against them since no one is immune to life's challenges.

For instance, offence may occur, misunderstandings could surface, and things might not work out as planned. However, staying with your partner during difficult times assures them of your love and commitment.

While adaptability keeps relationships stable, growth powers evolution. You and your partner should strive to develop and sail against stormy tides. Breaking a relationship or calling it quits because of challenges is never good. This would substantiate the maxim that a friend in need is a friend indeed.

Adaptability and growth are active concepts that require deliberate effort and a commitment to continuous learning and evolution. As a team, you must embrace life's journey and understand that change will come. If you both prepare against storms, you will smile through them when they arise.

Beyond reaching a destination, a flourishing relationship involves enjoying the journey together, constantly adapting, and adjusting as you navigate life's undulations.

Flexibility

Flexibility is adapting and adjusting our behaviours, expectations, and perspectives in response to changing circumstances. It does not mean you have to compromise your core values, but you must be empathetic, open-minded, and willing to negotiate.

Sometimes, a decision may only partially benefit you. However, flexibility requires you to sacrifice personal comfort for the corporate good. You may not always get everything you want in a relationship. However, with simplicity, you can find mutually agreeable solutions that balance your needs.

Besides, as people grow and change, so do their needs and desires. Expecting your partner to be the same as when you first met is unrealistic. Flexibility allows you to embrace these changes and adjust your expectations accordingly.

Again, you must be sensitive to situations where habits and patterns that once worked are no longer suitable. At such times, you need to reevaluate your behaviour and make adjustments where necessary.

Grudges and past grievances are what rust is to iron in every relationship. However, flexibility encourages us to let go of the past and forgive our partners. This will open the door to healing and reconciliation.

Let rigidity give way to flexibility. When you and your partner are willing to be flexible, it becomes less likely that you will reach an impasse.

More so, when your friend or spouse knows they can access and rely on you to be flexible, you win their trust and they feel secure. When partners can share their thoughts and feelings without fear of judgment or disapproval, they relate more honestly.

Your relationship will get stronger as much as you make your partner feel understood, accepted, and valued for who they are. Relationships that are built on flexibility are more likely to endure over time. Regardless of how hard the storm beats, it will be easier for you and your partner to adapt and adjust during tough times.

Growth and development are not negotiable in any relationship that will stand the test of time. Imagine how a fetus develops into a baby and the transitional processes from childhood to adolescence and adulthood. This continuous and stunning improvement should be reflected in any lasting relationship.

You can change an old car, dress, or shoe but can't change your spouse. They can't change you too. Although many people use divorce as an exit door from marriage, however, the emotional breakdown is heart-rending. The secret to lasting joy and the absence of boredom is continuous improvement. You must demonstrate positive shifts that will enthuse your partner.

Relationships should be active. As individuals grow, their connections should evolve positively, too. Continuous improvement enhances personal and relational growth. Thus, every relationship can remain relevant and fulfilling.

An excellent way to consistently work on yourself is to allow your partner to acknowledge imperfections and recognize areas needing attention. This evaluation will help you understand what to do. It will also help your spouse to work collaboratively with you towards solutions.

Continuous improvement is beyond addressing problems. If all you do is condemn and point out your partner's errors, you might do more harm than good.

You should also focus on celebrating strengths and acknowledging positive attributes. Appreciation strengthens mutual respect and renews the value of your union.

Handling Life Transition

Life is a journey filled with shifts and switches; big and small changes will evolve. Changing geographical location, coping with parenting responsibilities, switching jobs, dealing with increasing expenses, and many more events can test even the strongest relationships. The best approach is to handle situations jointly. Have you discovered that intimacy between partners gets more profound as they overcome challenges together?

The best way to sustain a relationship is to prepare for the worst situations. In some ways, this truth may be uncomfortable. But, you will hardly fail or give up if you factor in life transitions at the beginning of your relationship odyssey.

Dealing with uncertainties begins with an acknowledgement that they are inevitable. Change is the only constant there is.

To deal with these changes effectively, openly and honestly, talk about your fears, anxieties, and hopes when confronted with tough seasons in your relationship. Also, discuss how these changes will impact your lives individually and as a couple. Then, you can create actionable plans to navigate the challenges.

It is important to note that transitions require adjustments and sacrifices. You may need to spend less and invest more, for instance. This could mean cutting down expenses and streamlining luxuries.

Another reality for a family is having children to care for. The wife may need to spend more time with the children while the husband works to make ends meet. Working together allows you to adapt to the new reality and find ways to thrive. Effective communication will help you plan well and journey through with a high level of understanding.

"5 Pillars of Lasting Relationships" examines the fundamental principles that sustain every healthy relationship. From communication to trust, mutual respect to shared values, every chapter has provided valuable lessons to guide you toward achieving a lasting relationship.

It is essential to acknowledge that human relationships have inherent complexity. So, there is no 'one-size-fits-all' prescription for ensuring lasting partnership. It is so because every relationship is as unique as those who share it. However, by actuating the rudiments outlined in this book, we will become better equipped to nurture and sustain our most cherished relationships.

Furthermore, don't attempt to seek perfection as the key to a lasting relationship. Instead, focus on navigating the inevitable challenges and conflicts that usually arise along the way. You must be committed to honest and effective communication, willing to forgive and learn from past mistakes, and passionate about shared vision and collective success.

If conflict arises, see it as an opportunity for growth and transformation, and always remember the importance of togetherness and heartfelt moments. Conflicts can only last as long as you wish to keep them active. You have the power to quench it.

For every good relationship you build and sustain, you find solace, companionship, a profound sense of purpose, and fulfilment.

Let the insights and lessons you glean from this book serve as a compass as you navigate the complexity of human relationships. May you strive for genuine partnerships that stand the test of time and enrich your life beyond measure.